JOURNAL

of

PRAYER LETTERS

ELIZABETH GRIEST

Inks and Bindings
888-290-5218
www.inksandbindings.com
orders@inksandbindings.com

Contents

Dear Reader,

What follows are some prayer letters I have written.

The letters have helped me; I hope/pray they will help you, for; what can aid one can aid many.

Prayers/blessings,
Betsy Griest

I

Sacred Parents,

I need/ want things simple yet complete.

Thus, I believe my relationship with You is most important, followed by my relationship with myself, then, closely, my relationship with others.

Please bless me in all my relationships always/all ways.

Thank You, Mother/Father God of all.

_____
_____
_____
_____
_____
_____
_____
_____
_____
_____
_____
_____

II

Sacred Parents,

Help my inner child/me keep true to who I truly am/to my life purpose.

Help me recall/adhere to my Sacred life plan. Help me remember everyone has a Divine plan for his or her life.

Further, help me realize just how crucial the cooperation/partnership of one's child self is in grasping/following one's Divine destiny.

For the inner child is the holder of one's deepest feelings/beliefs about oneself/others/God as well as the holder of one's memories.

Too, the child self-arrives on earth clutching the blueprint of one's Divine destiny.

Feelings/Beliefs/Memories can all affect the living of/fulfillment of one's Sacred life plan.

Thus, one's inner child needs loving guidance/guardianship from one's adult self as well as from You, Sacred parents.

So, I believe.

Guide/guard my child self/me always/all ways.

Thank You, Divine Parents of us all.

_____
_____
_____
_____
_____
_____
_____
_____
_____
_____
_____
_____
_____
_____
_____
_____
_____
_____
_____
_____
_____
_____

III

Sacred Parents,

Please guide/guard always/all ways my physical health.

For we know how greatly affected I am—for good or ill—by diet, personal and household cleaners, air and water quality, climate.

Environments deeply affect me—physical as well as people. The latter particularly in their attitudes, emotions, words, voice tones, etc.

Everything/everyone impacts my physical health, which, in turn, affects my emotional/mental/spiritual wellbeing. Plus, of course, my ability to effectively grasp/execute portions of my life plan.

My high sensitivity is both my blessing and curse. Yet, said sensitivity is the bedrock of who I am.

After all, I could not hear You nor Your heavenly helpers, Your angels and spirit guides, without my sensitivity.

Aid in me being who I am while being helpful to myself and others and You.

For Divine Parents, I believe You do not need Your children's aid yet! Greatly desire it.

_____
_____
_____
_____
_____
_____
_____
_____
_____
_____
_____
_____
_____
_____
_____
_____
_____
_____
_____
_____
_____
_____

IV

Thank You, Sacred Parents, for Your insights/
guidance/support.

Divine Parents, I strongly suspect more individuals
are affected, in varying degrees, by physical/people
environments than the affected realize.

Guide/guard us all, Mother/Father of all. Thank You.

V

Sacred Parents,

We know how affected, for good or ill, I am by food.

We further know I cannot/do not give dietary advice that ultimately, I only can speak for myself. Yet, perhaps my experiences could benefit some individuals.

Thus, Divine Parents, please provide the best food and supplements for me. Please also impart the resolve to adhere to my diet as well as the flexibility to modify it when wise to do so.

Harmful foods can be so tempting/so addictive. Unfortunately, these foods are so prevalent.

Unfortunately too, such foods can be almost impossible to avoid when traveling/being dependent upon restaurants.

On those occasions, Divine Parents, assist me in recalling to take necessary extra supplements because bad or unwise foods can defocus me as well as exhaust me.

Sacred Parents, provide foods/beverages/ supplements that strengthen me physically/ emotionally/mentally/ spiritually.

Provide substances, which don't drain me and that don't result in anxiety/confusion/depression.

Thus, Parents of all, I need gluten-free/non-fried/non-chemical-based foods. I need as pure water as possible.

Further, I require as pure supplements as possible, particularly seaweed capsules, various herbal liquid extracts such as Nettle Leaf, purslane, the so-called garden weed plantain, nuts/seeds protein powder, apple cider vinegar, pure sea salt.

Guide/guard always/all ways.

Thank You, Sacred Parents.

_____
_____
_____
_____
_____
_____
_____
_____
_____
_____
_____
_____

VI

Sacred Parents,

Please guide/guard my inner child/me in Sacred self-care.

Please help her/me deeply know anything through You, including self-care, can never be selfish.

Thank You, Divine Parents.

Please help the living of my Sacred self-care be an integral part of living my Divine destiny.

Thank You, Parents of All.

_____
_____
_____
_____
_____
_____
_____
_____
_____
_____
_____
_____

VII

Sacred Parents,

Let there be a balanced blend of the spiritual with the practical in my life.

For I know both are essential.

Guide/guard me always/all ways.

Thank You, Parents of All.

_____
_____
_____
_____
_____
_____
_____
_____
_____
_____
_____
_____
_____
_____
_____

VIII

Sacred Parents,

Guide/guard my finances. Crystal clearly show me what to do as well as what not to do.

All so I can more completely live my Divine destiny.

Thank You.

_____

_____

_____

_____

_____

_____

_____

_____

_____

_____

_____

_____

_____

_____

_____

_____

_____

_____

IX

Sacred Parents,

I most know I'm actively living my Divine destiny when I feel/experience myself in Your Sacred free flow of inspirational ideas, inspirational information, inspirational events, inspirational circumstances, inspirational locations, and inspirational relationships.

_____

_____

_____

_____

_____

_____

_____

_____

_____

_____

_____

_____

_____

_____

_____

_____

_____

_____

X

Sacred Parents,

Please rule and cherish the universe now and forever.

_____
_____
_____
_____
_____
_____
_____
_____
_____
_____
_____
_____
_____
_____
_____
_____
_____
_____
_____
_____

XI

Sacred Parents,

Help me avoid bringing unhealthy food and beverages into my home. Help me to not consume bad food/bad beverages in restaurants.

I should say as much as possible, because stores and restaurants are usually loaded with unhealthy food and beverages. Healthy food and beverages are generally are far less—even sometimes in health food stores and restaurants.

Guide/guard me, please, Divine Parents.

Thank You.

_____
_____
_____
_____
_____
_____
_____
_____
_____
_____
_____

XII

Sacred Parents,

Bless me with the courage/stamina to live my life plan.

Yet, please make things as easy as possible.

Thank You, Divine Parents.

_____
_____
_____
_____
_____
_____
_____
_____
_____
_____
_____
_____
_____
_____
_____
_____
_____

XIII

Sacred Parents,

So often I simply need to declare—please, Divine Parents, take charge.

_____

_____

_____

_____

_____

_____

_____

_____

_____

_____

_____

_____

_____

_____

_____

_____

_____

_____

_____

_____

_____

XIV

Sacred Parents,

Be with me always/all ways. Thank You.

_____
_____
_____
_____
_____
_____
_____
_____
_____
_____
_____
_____
_____
_____
_____
_____
_____
_____
_____
_____
_____
_____

XV

Through You, Sacred Parents,

I take care of myself

I love myself

I help myself

I do what I love to do

I help those You guide me to.

_____

_____

_____

_____

_____

_____

_____

_____

_____

_____

_____

_____

_____

XVI

Sacred Parents,

You are Mother/Father God of all.

From You/in You, my child self/I live/move/ Have my being,

Sacred Parents, you know how fearful my inner child/I can feel, how overwhelmed she/I can be by the complexities/ complications of the world with its multitude of circumstances/perplexities/personalities.

Ever hold us close as You guide/guard my child self/me through this life.

Thank You, Divine parents.

_____
_____
_____
_____
_____
_____
_____
_____
_____

XVII

Keeping close to You, Divine Parents, is my true protection and provision while knowing any trouble/any lack I may experience still draws me closer to You. Even when I cannot see that for some time.

But always, I ask You to guide me away from/guard me from all suffering.

Unless some suffering is truly necessary for my soul growth.

_____

_____

_____

_____

_____

_____

_____

_____

_____

_____

_____

_____

_____

_____

XVIII

Sacred Parents,

Your Sacred healing for all!

Your Sacred peace and plenty for all!

All means every person, plant, animal.

Thank You, Divine Parents of all.

_____
_____
_____
_____
_____
_____
_____
_____
_____
_____
_____
_____
_____
_____
_____

XIX

Sacred Parents,

I need You so. I have so many fears. Calm/comfort me.

Guide/guard me.

Hold me close in Your infinite love for me.

Thank You.

_____

_____

_____

_____

_____

_____

_____

_____

_____

_____

_____

_____

_____

_____

XX

Sacred Parents,

Help me believe in myself while honoring other's beliefs in themselves.

Above all, Divine Parents, help me believe in, honor You.

Thank You, Parents of us all.

_____
_____
_____
_____
_____
_____
_____
_____
_____
_____
_____
_____
_____
_____
_____

XXI

Sacred Parents,

Please make my life such that I need to utilize mostly my strengths and very little of my weaknesses.

For the most part, I'm healthier/happier when using mainly my strengths while not having to deal with my weaknesses.

Understand/guide/guard me, please, Divine Parents. Thank You.

XXII

Sacred Parents,

Through Your Sacred freedom, I claim my Sacred good.

Through Your Sacred power, I share my Sacred good with others,

Thank You, Sacred Parents.

_____
_____
_____
_____
_____
_____
_____
_____
_____
_____
_____
_____
_____
_____
_____

XXIII

Sacred Parents,

Through Your Sacred freedom, I am free to express my true self.

Yes, via ways that honor myself/others/You, Divine Parents.

Thank You, Mother/Father of all.

_____

_____

_____

_____

_____

_____

_____

_____

_____

_____

_____

_____

_____

_____

_____

XXIV

Through You, Sacred Parents, I allow my inner child/myself to be healed/freed of false/hurtful beliefs about myself/You/others.

_____

_____

_____

_____

_____

_____

_____

_____

_____

_____

_____

_____

_____

_____

_____

_____

_____

_____

_____

_____

_____

XXV

Sacred Parents,

Help me for I so often feel too weak physically/mentally/emotionally spiritually to go on.

Help me for I so often feel too bogged down by my mistakes to go on.

Hold me in Your arms, reassure me of Your everlasting love for all Your children, including me.

Thank You, Parents of us all.

_____

_____

_____

_____

_____

_____

_____

_____

_____

_____

_____

_____

XXVI

Sacred Parents,

For all the tragic loss Your children have suffered, please, Sacred resolution.

From my experience and observation, sometimes resolution comes via Your Divine equivalent, not always through Divine duplication.

Still, Parents of all, still, prevent painful loss as much as possible. Thank You, Mother/Father God.

_____

_____

_____

_____

_____

_____

_____

_____

_____

_____

_____

_____

_____

XXVII

Sacred Parents,

Help me live my strengths as often/as much as possible.

Help me heal my weaknesses. Help me transform them into strengths. All the while, protect me from perfectionism.

For I believe, only You are perfect.

At the same time, Divine Parents, You help Your children grow ever deeper in Sacred strength/love for themselves/others/You.

Thank You, Parents of all.

_____
_____
_____
_____
_____
_____
_____
_____
_____

XXVIII

Sacred Parents,

When I'm called upon to aid those I do not resonate well with, please help me do so as courteously/clearly/completely as possible, as quickly too.

The same holds true for communicating with individuals I don't resonate well with.

Also, assist me in being empathetic/prayerful for all.

Thank You, Parents of all.

_____

_____

_____

_____

_____

_____

_____

_____

_____

_____

_____

_____

XXIX

Sacred Parents,

Please help me not be rattled, knocked off center/thrown off kilter by difficult personalities.

Instead, please enable me to be centered in You as well as in healthy self-esteem.

Please, Divine Parents.

Thank You.

XXX

Sacred Parents,

You know/You show anything/anyone I need to know, be shown.

Thank You, Divine Parents.

_____
_____
_____
_____
_____
_____
_____
_____
_____
_____
_____
_____
_____
_____
_____
_____
_____
_____

XXXI

Sacred Parents,

Sometimes I can't help but feel You don't love me or love me enough or love me in the ways most important to me. The ways I most want/need.

You understand. You do not chide me.

You help me hold on to You in faith.

Help me always/all ways hold onto You, Divine Parents.

_____
_____
_____
_____
_____
_____
_____
_____
_____
_____
_____
_____

XXXII

Sacred Parents,

Your Sacred timing for Your complete Sacred healing/Your complete Sacred peace/Your complete Sacred plenty for all!

Please!

Thank You, Divine Parents.

XXXIII

Sacred Parents,

Your total Grace and Mercy for all!

Thank You, Divine Parents.

_____

_____

_____

_____

_____

_____

_____

_____

_____

_____

_____

_____

_____

_____

_____

_____

_____

_____

_____

_____

_____

XXXIV

Sacred Parents,

Your Sacred forgiveness/Your Sacred release for all!

Please!

Thank You, Divine Parents.

_____
_____
_____
_____
_____
_____
_____
_____
_____
_____
_____
_____
_____
_____
_____
_____
_____
_____
_____
_____
_____

XXXV

Sacred Parents,

Your Sacred reconciliation for all!

Please!

Thank You, Divine Parents.

_____
_____
_____
_____
_____
_____
_____
_____
_____
_____
_____
_____
_____
_____
_____
_____
_____
_____

XXXVI

Sacred Parents,

Even when I can't love others because of the pain they cause me,

Even when I can't love myself because I can't love others,

Even then, Divine Parents, love me! And, thus, help me love others. Please!

For I know You desire all Your children to love one another.

Thank You, Sacred Parents of us all.

_____

_____

_____

_____

_____

_____

_____

_____

_____

_____

_____

XXXVII

Sacred Parents,

Enable/empower all Your children to discover/live his/her Sacred life purpose.

Thank You, Divine Parents of us all.

_____

_____

_____

_____

_____

_____

_____

_____

_____

_____

_____

_____

_____

_____

_____

_____

_____

_____

_____

_____

_____

XXXVIII

Sacred Parents,

When I am overwhelmed/overwrought by confusion/anxiety/depression/exhaustion, You mercifully do not burden me with pious platitudes.

Rather, You mercifully provide comfort/ encouragement/reassurance. Plus, insights with practical step-by-step healing guidance all under Your omnipresent/omnipotent guardianship.

Thank You, Blessed Divine Parents.

I know You can/will do such for all Your children.

Sometimes we children need to ask You to do so, other times, super mercifully we don't even have to ask.

XXXIX

Sacred Parents,

Bless me always/all ways with Your Sacred love/Your Sacred wisdom.

Guide/guard me always/all ways with Your sacred love/Your Sacred wisdom.

Thank You.

_____
_____
_____
_____
_____
_____
_____
_____
_____
_____
_____
_____
_____
_____
_____
_____
_____

XL

Sacred Parents,

Please help me!

Thank You, Blessed Parents, for I have faith,
know You will.

_____

_____

_____

_____

_____

_____

_____

_____

_____

_____

_____

_____

_____

_____

_____

_____

_____

_____

XLI

Sacred security/Sacred health/Sacred self-fulfillment for myself as well as for others.

Via You, Divine Parents.

Thank You.

_____
_____
_____
_____
_____
_____
_____
_____
_____
_____
_____
_____
_____
_____
_____
_____
_____
_____

XLII

Sacred Parents,

Grant me nightly peaceful slumber for its lack can greatly denigrate my physical/mental/emotional/spiritual wellbeing.

Help me be especially careful of what I'm ingesting physically/mentally/emotionally/spiritually because all can deeply impact my wellbeing for ill or for good.

Guide/guard me always/all ways.

Thank You, Divine Parents.

_____

_____

_____

_____

_____

_____

_____

_____

_____

_____

_____

_____

XLIII

⤙⤙✦⤛⤛

My inner child/I possess Your permission,
Sacred Parents, to joyfully/completely live our
Divine destiny.

Thank You, Divine Parents of all.

_____

_____

_____

_____

_____

_____

_____

_____

_____

_____

_____

_____

_____

_____

_____

_____

_____

_____

XLIV

Sacred Parents,

Help my child self/me retain my awe of You, yet, not fear.

Because You are the ever-loving/ever-present Mama/Papa of all.

Mama/Papa God, help me be centered/anchored in You.

Thank You, Sacred Parents.

_____
_____
_____
_____
_____
_____
_____
_____
_____
_____
_____
_____

XLV

Mama/ Papa God!

You know how my inner child/I partially resent certain tasks/roles, which have fallen upon me.

Thank You, Sacred Parents, that You do not shame/blame/guilt me for my pain/resentment.

Rather, You gently help me see/remember/focus upon the good/growth these tasks/roles have fostered.

_____
_____
_____
_____
_____
_____
_____
_____
_____
_____
_____
_____
_____

XLVI

Sacred Parents,

I believe You want all Your children to be true noblemen and noblewomen of the soul.

An aristocracy not based upon titles, formal education, money, worldly power but rooted in genuine courtesy/fairness/mercy.

Help all Your children be/live as spiritual aristocrats.

Thank You, Mama/Papa of all.

_____

_____

_____

_____

_____

_____

_____

_____

_____

_____

_____

_____

XLVII

Mama/Papa God,

Please provide the right/resonant people and circumstances for my child self's/my continual soul growth.

Dear God, please make the process as comfortable as possible.

Mama/Papa God, as an added benefit, please provide some souls and situations to whom/where I can safely express part of my pixie playfulness. What a blessing that would be.

Thank You, Beloved Mama/Papa of all.

_____
_____
_____
_____
_____
_____
_____
_____
_____
_____
_____

XLVIII

Sacred Parents,

You can be known in Your total essence of love.

Yet, You possess/impart a myriad of marvelous mysteries.

Mysteries for Your children to ponder/pray about, should they choose to.

So I believe, Divine Parents.

_____

_____

_____

_____

_____

_____

_____

_____

_____

_____

_____

_____

_____

XLIX

Mother/Mama/Father/Papa God,

One of Your greatest mysteries, I find, is Your Divine femaleness/Divine maleness. Therefore, Your children's human femaleness/human maleness.

Especially the latter can be quite mysterious, at least from my perspective.

_____

_____

_____

_____

_____

_____

_____

_____

_____

_____

_____

_____

_____

_____

_____

_____

_____

_____

L

Sacred Parents,

It so often calms/centers me to enter into Your Sacred meditative free flow of Sacred words such as:

Sacred synchronicities

Sacred security

Sacred situations

Sacred relationships

Help me ever more deeply ponder/pray about Your holy words.

_____

_____

_____

_____

_____

_____

_____

_____

_____

_____

LI

Mama/Papa God of all,

Help me be ever grateful for Your belief in me, especially when I couldn't believe in myself.

And like unto it, help me be ever grateful for Your children who believed in me particularly when I couldn't.

Aid me, Divine Parents, to always express gratitude for Your Sacred support emanating from You, and Your children.

Thank You.

Your child,
Betsy

LII

Sacred Parents,

Help me be grateful for my strengths, my abilities, things I've done well.

Just as importantly, help me be grateful for my weaknesses, my lack of various abilities, things I've botched.

For there's been/is learning/growth on both sides of the scales.

Help my gratitude be extended to others for their strengths, abilities, things they've done well. Just as importantly also, help my gratitude be extended to others for their weaknesses, lack of various abilities, their blunders.

For there's been/is learning/growth on both sides of the scales for us all.

Help us all learn/grow in Your love for all.

Your child,
Betsy